THE OFFICIAL BOOK

STEPS

First published in 1999 by Virgin Books,
an imprint of Virgin Publishing Ltd
Thames Wharf Studios,
Rainville Road, London W6 9HT

A catalogue record for the book is available from the British Library.

ISBN 1 85227 851 X

Printed and bound by The Bath Press, Bath

Colour Origination by Colourwise Ltd

Designed by Slatter~Anderson

THE OFFICIAL BOOK

JORDAN PARAMOR

Virgin

Contents

It's bright and brilliant, and brimming with loads of fantastic facts that you never knew before! Find out how we all felt at the Steps auditions, where we like to go on holiday, the best (and the worst!) Christmas presents we've ever been given, the most unusual traditions we've come across as we've travelled the world, and tons more. This book is packed with top gossip, exclusive interviews and never-been-seen-before pictures – some taken by none other than that master photographer H!

Over the past couple of years we've had the time of our lives. We never dreamed that all this would happen – it's incredible! So we want to take this opportunity to say a massive thanks to all of you for supporting us, and to tell you that the best is still to come! We hope you enjoy this book as much as we enjoyed putting it together, and we look forward to seeing you all soon!

Lisa
X

CAST YOUR MINDS BACK TO NOVEMBER 1997,
WHEN, AS IF FROM NOWHERE, THE BAND THAT
WERE TO BECOME BRITAIN'S BIGGEST NEW POP
PHENOMENON APPEARED.

Step One :

The Beginning

Trussed up in matching brightly coloured outfits, they grabbed the attention of the nation when they released the line dancing extravaganza "5, 6, 7, 8." But while this was the public's first glimpse of the band with the brightest smiles in pop, the guys and gals themselves had been working hard for months, preparing to launch themselves on the fun-loving public.

The story begins way back in May 1997, when a gap was spotted in the music market for a mixed boy/girl band. The charts were awash with all-girl and all-boy bands, and pop lovers were crying out for something different. Soon they were going to get it.

An advert was placed in showbiz paper The Stage advertising for "Young, fit, talented, good looking people." Applications came rolling in, and soon the first set of auditions took place.

H was the first member to be chosen. Having previously worked as a Children's Entertainer at Butlins, he was a natural performer, and as well as displaying impressive singing and dancing skills, he had the whole room in stitches from the word go. "I'm not exactly shy am I?" he laughs, "And I ended up talking to just about everyone I came into contact with. I don't even know what I was talking to them about!"

Dressed in jeans and a big black-and-white fluffy jumper, he swallowed his nerves and gave it his best shot. As he explains, "Everyone else was in leg warmers and tights looking really professional, and I hadn't even had any We all lined up and were given numbers to pin on our tops, then we had to dance and sing. I did a bit of line dancing, which was really odd, then I sang " Things Can Only Get Better" by D:ream and the theme tune from *Starlight Express*. Then we had to talk about ourselves for two minutes. Although obviously I talked for a little bit longer than two minutes!"

No surprise there, then!

Contents

HURRAH! A BIG HELLO AND WELCOME TO THE FIRST OFFICIAL STEPS BOOK!

It's bright and brilliant, and brimming with loads of fantastic facts that you never knew before! Find out how we all felt at the Steps auditions, where we like to go on holiday, the best (and the worst!) Christmas presents we've ever been given, the most unusual traditions we've come across as we've travelled the world, and tons more. This book is packed with top gossip, exclusive interviews and never-been-seen-before pictures – some taken by none other than that master photographer H!

Over the past couple of years we've had the time of our lives. We never dreamed that all this would happen – it's incredible! So we want to take this opportunity to say a massive thanks to all of you for supporting us, and to tell you that the best is still to come! We hope you enjoy this book as much as we enjoyed putting it together, and we look forward to seeing you all soon!

Lisa was the next to secure her place in the supergroup after making certain she got noticed. A graduate of the famous Italia Conti stage school in London, she'd already sung and danced her way around the world, and at the time was singing with a three-piece girl band called The Leslie Curtis Affair. That day, dressed in grey tracksuit bottoms and a pink cropped top with a big blue heart on (which she's kept to this day), she marched straight to the front of the audition and volunteered to sing first. After belting out the Alannah Myles rock number "Black Velvet," she displayed her enviable dancing skills while shimmying to an early version of "5, 6, 7, 8." Then she went home and crossed her fingers. Two days later, on her 21st birthday, she got a phone call. She was in.

"I was so excited I phoned my family and friends and said, 'I'm in a line dancing pop group!' I think they were a bit worried about the line dancing bit. But then again, so was I! I wrote in my diary that "5, 6, 7, 8" was extremely tacky so it would probably be a hit.

"I can't knock it though, because it launched us worldwide and got us where

we are today. But I was worried because I thought it would either be a massive hit or a huge flop. I'd wanted to be a pop star for years, and I didn't want to be a one hit – or worse – a no hit wonder!"

But there was no chance of that. All they had to do was find three more band members and they were away. So a second set of auditions were held, and H and Lisa were given the task of helping to find the perfect performers. They had to have style, talent and a huge dollop of personality. The race was on to find the perfect contenders…

Claire drove to the auditions, getting totally lost in the process. But luckily she had her sister – who she'd brought along for moral support – to calm her nerves. The poor lass was so terrified that she nearly didn't go, but in the end it was her mum who encouraged her to go for her dreams. Claire had been temping doing secretarial work for the previous seven months, but her real love was singing, and her mum knew she had the talent to make it.

Having already been a member of all-girl pop band T.S.D., Claire knew what to expect from the auditions. She'd toured with Boyzone, Peter Andre and Ant and Dec, but that didn't stop her visibly shaking when it came to the crunch.

"I was fine with the singing, but I was really worried about dancing." says Claire, reliving the memory.

"It takes me ages to pick up dance routines. Once I know it I can do it, but it takes me a while to learn. I was really hoping they'd do the singing first, but instead we had to line dance. It was so scary!"

But Claire needn't have worried. Wearing the catsuit she wears in the "Last Thing On My Mind" video, she made it through the dancing and went on to stun everyone with her voice when she sang Tina Turner's "River Deep Mountain High" – which she'd learnt the night before – and Eternal's "I Am Blessed". In fact, she made such an impression that the rest of the band could hear her singing three rooms away. "I was stunned!" laughs Faye.

Once she'd got through the trauma of performing, Claire had something else scary to contend with. "They were dwindling people down and they called out my name and number. But there was another girl called Claire with a similar number to me and we both stepped forward. I froze, but then Tim pointed to me and said *that* Claire. I couldn't believe it!"

She immediately ran down the corridor and hugged her sister, and was so excited she offered everyone else in the band a lift home without even knowing where they lived!

The Steps story could have been very different had it not been for Lee's determination. He became concerned when he didn't hear back after sending his CV and photo off to co-manager Tim Byrne. But not one to give up easily, Lee called his office and was disappointed to discover that his application never actually arrived. Luckily they told him to come along to the auditions anyway.

Being a graduate of The Laine Theatre School in Epsom, he'd had plenty of performing experience, so he wasn't too nervous when he turned up wearing his white jeans, black top and trainers. It also helped that some of his mates from college were also auditioning, so they could keep each other calm.

Lee was also on his third audition for *Tommy* in London's West End, so if things didn't work out he was hoping he'd have that to fall back on. But as we all know, he didn't need a back-up plan because he was an obvious choice for the steadily growing band. After some expert dancing and a rendition of Take That's "Back For Good" and Patrick Swayze's "She's Like The Wind," his place was secured.

BUT IT DIDN'T ALL RUN SMOOTHLY, AS LEE TELLS US.

"I got down to the last two boys and then I started to really worry. When I realised I had a good chance of getting in I decided I really wanted it, so I started to get a bit nervous. But thankfully I got in, and I immediately phoned my mum and told her – she was so proud of me!"

And what mum wouldn't be?

In the days before Steps, Faye was the resident singer at London's swanky Hilton hotel, crooning each night in what she describes as "my Crystal Barbie outfit"! But when she saw the Steps ad in *The Stage*, she saw her dreams of pop stardom flash in front of her face and she set about applying.

When she arrived at the audition wearing some coppery trousers and a white vest top, she was stunned by the amount of people there – about 600 in all! But she sailed though her dancing audition, having done line dancing before. "When I worked as an entertainer in a hotel, I used to teach people line dancing to 'Achy Breaky Heart'," she giggles. But she decided against singing the Billy Ray Cyrus classic at the audition, and instead plumped for M People and Celine Dion numbers. But then she found herself facing the same nightmare as Lee and Claire.

"They'd narrowed us down to the final few, and they had this other girl called Kim from a previous audition there just in case she fitted in." Faye says, "That's when I thought I hadn't got in – because she had a bigger chest than I did! But I found out at four o'clock on 7 May 1997 that I'd got it, and I immediately phoned my mum. I was so excited!"

With the last member in place, the band was complete and ready to rock the charts. So with dreams of a record deal and worldwide stardom, the fivesome joined together and put their best foot forward...

They didn't have to wait long for a deal to come along.

They were swiftly signed to Ebul, legendary producer and writer Pete Waterman's label. The label is affiliated to Jive records, home of Backstreet Boys and Britney Spears, so they knew they had a good team behind them. After perfecting the 5, 6, 7, 8 hoedown, they set to work touring the country's under-18s clubs performing "5, 6, 7, 8".

Claire laughs as she tells the story. "We spent three months touring clubs and doing under-18s discos. We were still getting to know each other and we had a right laugh, but we got a bit bored of wearing our red costumes all the time. People must have thought we were really smelly!"

Although they went down a storm on the tour, they still had their reservations about how their debut single would go. But as Lee explains, they all tried to stay positive. "I thought 'we're all here, we've all got the same goals and ambitions and we're all giving it a go.' And we knew that whatever happened, no-one could put us down for trying."

"5, 6, 7, 8" was put out just in time for it to become a stomping Christmas party hit. It peaked at number 14, and stayed in the charts for the next three months. An appearance at the *Smash Hits* Poll Winners Party followed, giving the band a chance to reach a nationwide audience. "We were in awe that day," Faye says excitedly, "There were so many celebrities there and I didn't know where to look. Gary Barlow said hello to us, and Ronan from Boyzone waved, and Celine Dion came up and told me that she liked my hair! I was in a dream world, flabbergasted.

"IT WAS THE BIGGEST BUZZ GOING ON STAGE AND SEEING ALL THE PEOPLE WATCHING US AS WELL. JUST LITTLE OLD US ON THIS HUGE STAGE. IT WAS SUCH A BLUR THAT WHEN WE CAME OFF WE WANTED TO GO BACK ON AND HAVE ANOTHER GO!"

And they got their chance. Just a year later, in 1998, they closed the show as all the other artists joined them on stage to sing "Tragedy." It was the finale to end all finales.

After the success of "5, 6, 7, 8" there was no stopping Steps. The pop gem "Last Thing On My Mind" was released in April 1998 and hit the number six spot. It became a massive club hit, and made Steps a band to watch. London bible *Time Out* described it as "Summer's first great pop song," while snoot industry mag *Music Week* made it their single of the week.

The vivacious ballad "One For Sorrow" was released in August '98 and dived into the number two spot. Next came the double A-sided track "Heartbeat/Tragedy", which secured the number one spot after a whopping eight weeks, sold 1.4 million copies (making it the biggest selling Bee Gees single ever), and stayed in the charts for over six months. "Better Best Forgotten" – the last single off their debut album *Step One* – came next and reached number two.

The band's fears of being a one hit wonder were well and truly over!

You've got the album, you love the single, now dance along with our Step by Step guide to...

5 , 6 , 7 , 8

1

Adopt a big smile and take two steps to the right.
Do a high clap to the right.

2a

Keep smiling, repeat to the left!

Repeat steps one and two.

2b

3

Place your hands on your hips and swing your hips
in a circle to the left, then to the right.

Step to the right, stretching your right arm out 'n' up in front of you, and slap your bottom with your other hand as you step!

4

Repeat to your left hand side!

5

6a

Clasp your hands together and point to your left, taking a little jump back.

Repeat on your right hand side!

6b

Raise your right arm in the air and hold your left arm in front of your chest. Turn around anticlockwise punching the air as you go! Ta-da! You're a 5, 6, 7, Expert!

7

THE STEPS GANG ALWAYS SEEM SO CLOSE, BUT WAS IT
ALWAYS THAT WAY? HERE THEY REVEAL THEIR FIRST
IMPRESSIONS OF EACH OTHER, AND HOW THEIR FRIENDSHIPS
HAVE CHANGED ALONG THE WAY.

Back To You Guys!

H

"I thought H was really laddy and cool when I first met him!" Faye laughs as she talks about the maddest member of Steps. The others agree that they also got the wrong impression of H at first. "I thought he was cool and trendy and sensible. How wrong was I?" says a flabbergasted Lee. Very!

"I didn't realise just how bonkers he was!" says Claire, "But then I got to know him and I couldn't believe what he used to say and do. But he got away with it all because he was so cheeky!"

H and Lisa were in the band for a while before the others, so they shared a special bond from the word go – despite the fact that Lisa initially thought H was rude! "He was talking to everyone else and he ignored me, but then I realised that he was just in his own world.

"But after that we got on brilliantly because we were both Welsh and had a similar sense of humour. We've always had a special friendship."

When it came to habits, not surprisingly H had a fair few unusual ones which shocked his fellow band members. As Faye explains, "He did this thing where it'd be totally silent and all of a sudden he'd let out this massive burst of laughter for no reason! The first time he did it I thought he was a bit odd, but it made me laugh so much that I was crying. He was always winding us up and acting like a nutter so it took a little while to get used to him!"

"He was like a kid," Lee says rolling his eyes, "Whenever we travelled anywhere he'd be going, 'Are we nearly there yet? I need the toilet!' He couldn't sit still for a minute."

So how have the bands opinions changed since they first set eyes on the blonde bombshell?

"I though H was really crazy and wild, but underneath he's a really, really great guy. I didn't think he'd be the one to remember everyone's birthdays and stuff, but he's really brilliant."

Claire adds, "We all love him, but we know he's not the cool, smooth guy we all thought he was at the beginning! He's a nutter!"

CLAIRE

"Claire will kill me for saying this, but when I first saw her I thought she was about 29 or 30 because she had really short hair and she acted really grown up," H whispers cheekily, recalling the first time he saw the lovely Claire at the auditions.

"And she fancied me of course. All the girls did, obviously!

"But what really struck everyone about Claire was her incredible voice – and, er, her catsuit!"

"She sounded amazing. I remember thinking, 'Crikey, she's got some lungs on her!'" Faye laughs.

"And she was wearing this really nice blue stripy catsuit and I thought she looked great," says Lisa. "The first thing I said to her when she got into the band was, 'Excellent, now I can borrow your catsuit!'"

Lee still feels grateful towards Claire for giving him a lift home after the audition even though she didn't know him. But things didn't run totally smoothly between them from there. "Claire was always late." Lee laughs, "I'm always right on time and I like everything to be organised, and she was so disorganised. It became a standing joke between us, and luckily it didn't affect our friendship."

Faye was the first Stepster Claire bonded with, after Faye stayed over at her house a few times – her mum even did some of Faye's washing! But Lisa soon joined them and the trio had a girlie night over at Claire's, becoming firm friends after staying up the entire night talking.

"We had such a laugh together and got on brilliantly." says Lisa. "Claire's a brilliant listener and I'll chat to her whenever I've got a problem."

But has Claire changed since their initial meeting? Faye reckons not at all.

"CLAIRE'S ALWAYS BEEN COSY AND HOMELY AND SHE'S STILL THE SAME NOW, SHE'S GREAT." "BUT SHE'S STILL NOT ON TIME!" QUIPS LEE.

FAYE

The first thing everyone noticed about Faye was her blonde hair and huge smile. "She really stood out because she had this great curly blonde hair and she was really lively," says Lee.

Claire thought she was a dead cert to get into the band. "I spotted Faye straight away because she's so pretty, and I remember thinking, 'If she can sing, she's in.'"

"SHE WAS ALL SMILEY AND CURLY AND GENUINE,

AND SHE LOOKED REALLY GLAMOROUS," H SAYS.

"She was a really good dancer as well, so I thought she had a good chance of getting in." Little did H know that Faye was in awe of him and Lisa. "They were already in the band and I looked at them and thought, 'They're pop stars, they are!'" she laughs.

But while Lisa agreed that Faye was fab, she had one big worry. "I thought she was too tall because I was so small. Also in the beginning she used to wear high heels a lot so I looked titchy, but luckily she doesn't any more!"

As well as bonding with Claire at the beginning, Faye also hit it off with Lee. "I spoke to Faye on the day of the auditions and I thought she was a really nice girl. She's very level-headed and grown up, so I got on really well with her. I go to her a lot when I've got problems these days. She always knows the right things to say."

Do the band reckon that their first impressions of Faye were right?

"Yep, she's still curly and smiley!" H says sweetly.

LISA

Everyone thought Lisa was really cool and glamorous the first time they set eyes on her – she stole the show when she walked into Claire, Lee and Faye's audition. "She was wearing a bright orange dress, had a brilliant tan, really long dark hair and platforms. She looked like a proper pop star!" Faye remembers.

CLAIRE SAYS THAT "SHE WAS REALLY FRIENDLY," WHILE LEE THOUGHT SHE WAS REALLY KIND BECAUSE SHE LOOKED AFTER HIS BAG AS HE SLOGGED THROUGH HIS AUDITION.

Lisa was still working for the first month that the band was together, but she soon settled in and was having the time of her life.

Because she and H had been picked for the band a while before the others, they'd already become good mates, but she got to know all about Lee quickly when she moved in with the two fellas for a little while. "It was a laugh," Lisa says, "But H and I were really slobby and Lee's *so* tidy!" Everyone learnt early on that if they wanted to party, Lisa was the girl to go to. "She was always bounding around in search of a party, and you could always jump on the bandwagon with her," Faye admits.

But is Lisa still the friendly, glamorous party girl they all believed she was? "Oh yes!" reveals Claire, "No-one likes to party more than Lisa!"

LEE

Steps' resident hunk caught everyone's eye when he attended the auditions. Not only do they all describe him as "The best looking bloke in the room," but he was incredibly polite, and the first person to go up and talk to H.

The two lads hit it off immediately. "Lee was ideal for the band because he was the total opposite of me. He was really calm and sensible, and yet we really got on."

"I thought Lee was a nice genuine guy," says Lisa. "I overheard him phoning his mum to let her know how he was getting on, and at the end of the conversation he told her he loved her. I thought it was so sweet!"

But there was one thing about Lee that everyone thought was funny. "He was so over-tidy. For a bloke that looked a bit laddy it didn't seem normal. One time at the beginning we all went round to his house to watch a video and I dropped some popcorn on the floor. He literally followed me around picking it up. I couldn't believe it!" Faye giggles.

"He was so neat that his room looked like everything had been measured out with a ruler, it was bizarre!" H reveals. And although they can laugh about it now, Lee and Claire used to bicker like brother and sister.

"Lee and I always used to disagree because we both think we're always right. Although generally I am!" laughs Claire. All four other members of Steps reckon they were pretty spot on with their first impressions of Lee.

"HE'S STILL REALLY TIDY AND A GREAT SHOULDER TO LEAN ON. HE HASN'T CHANGED A BIT," SAYS LISA.

HOW DO THEY GET ON NOW?

Lisa: "I don't think our relationship has changed that much. We've always got on well and I think we always will. We've been through so much together that there's a special bond between us now."

H: "We bonded immediately and I think we've stood the test of time. This is such a hard business to get through and remain friends, but we have. I think if we can stay friends through this then we can stay friends through anything."

Faye: "They've actually become my best friends. To begin with I wasn't sure whether we'd become friends or just be work associates. But we've got to know each other so well, we know each other's funny habits and we've got a kind of brother/sister relationship. We can scrap when we want and forget it five minutes later."

Lee: "We're still finding out new things about each other every day. It's like… we're best friends and we have a brilliant time together, but we're only human!"

Claire: "We know what each other is thinking these days because we're together so much. When we're not working we do allow each other to have a life out of the band and we'll go off and do our own thing – but we do meet up for a good night out! There was never a case of us not getting on. I think we all feel the same as when we first met and we still like each other a lot. I don't think that will ever change."

Claire

When were you born?

17th August 1977

Where were you born?

Hillingdon, Middlesex

What time were you born?

1.30am

What's the naughtiest thing you did at school?

I was a bit of a goody two-shoes at school, but one day I went out with my friends at lunchtime to get some chips without a lunch pass. My friends used to do it every day, but I did it once and got caught!

What was the first item of clothing you bought?

I came up to London with my mum and I bought a pair of really baggy jeans. Really baggy.

What was your favourite/least favourite subject at school?

My favourite was P.E., and I really liked pottery. But I hated R.E. and I never saw the point of it.

Who was your best friend at school?

I had different ones all the time. I used to change every year and hang out with different people so I didn't have a proper best friend.

Where did you used to hang out with your mates?

At the tennis courts of Brunel University. We'd all play tennis, then get bored and go and watch the boys playing football!

What was your first taste of showbiz?

I got the lead part in *The Sound Of Music* when I was at school. I also used to do karaoke competitions, but I got barred from the local pub competition because I kept winning! I did win the inter-brewery competition, though.

Who was the first celebrity you met?

I met the Irish comedian Frank Carson when he did a show at our local theatre. And I also met Michael Barrymore when I auditioned for *The Barrymore Show!*

When did you get your ears pierced?

When I was seven at a market stall. It really hurt.

What was the first record you bought?

"Into The Groove" by Madonna.

Which celebrity did you have your first crush on?

Rick Astley. I thought he was gorgeous and I loved his voice. I was in love with Jordan Knight from New Kids On The Block as well.

What did you want to be when you were young?

Rich and famous! I wanted to be in musicals. But before that I wanted to be a beautician and a chef!

What colour is your bath towel at home?

Lemon yellow.

What's your duvet like?

It's white with green swirls on.

What's your favourite TV programme?

Friends, Top Of The Pops and *CD:UK*.

What's your favourite kind of fish?

I don't really like fish, but I'll eat battered cod from a fish and chip shop, or lobster!

What's your favourite flower?

White lilies.

What's the most expensive thing you've ever bought?

My car, it's a Suzuki Vitara jeep.

What's your biggest regret?

Not getting famous quicker, hahaha! Seriously though, I never regret anything.

What's your biggest triumph?

Steps.

What makes you laugh until you cry?

My sister, and stupid things like if someone falls over.

Who was the last person you fancied?

I think Kevin from Backstreet Boys is lovely. He's got very thin lips, but the rest of him is lovely!

What's the weirdest rumour you've heard about yourself?

That I'm going out with Lee. That one did the rounds for quite a while.

How long do you take to get ready?

I can get ready really quickly, but generally I take hours because I'm really lazy. I'll mess around and start getting ready three hours before I'm going out and still not be ready!

Who's your favourite Disney character?

The Little Mermaid.

What do you always carry around in your bag?

My purse, my filofax, a pen, a tube of Carmex, cough sweets, my keys, a compact and half a packet of chewing gum.

How do you have your tea?

I don't, I hate tea.

How much sleep do you need?

A lot. I'm useless if I don't get enough sleep.

What can't you live without?

My family, because if it wasn't for my mum I'd look like a tramp!

Have you got a special teddy?

I've got two. One that was given to me the day I was born, he's called Honey. And I've got a little elephant that I carry with me on the road and cuddle when I go to sleep if I'm feeling lonely.

What do you hope no-one ever finds out?

I've got nothing bad for anyone to find out, I've always been a good girl!

Tell us a secret!

I used to eat crackerbread with sugar on, and Branston pickle on toast.

THERE'S NOTHING THE STEPSTERS LIKE MORE THAN A GOOD RELAXING HOLIDAY AND THE CHANCE TO GET A TAN. JOIN THEM AS THEY PACK THEIR BAGS AND HEAD FOR THE SUN!

The First Thing On Their Minds!

Holiday Time

Where did you used to go on holiday when you were a kid?

Faye: Camping around England. I didn't mind it, but I didn't like the outside toilets because there were always daddy-longlegs in there!

Lisa: We always went to Tenerife because we had a place out there.

H: We used to go to Barry Island and Pontins and other holiday camps. We went to Arcudia in Spain once and it was terrible. We were in a one-star hotel and we all ate goulash and got holiday tummy. Never eat goulash in Spain, that's my tip!

Lee: I've never been abroad with my parents. Instead we used to go to Wales and stay in a caravan by the beach every year. It was great fun!

Claire: We always went somewhere different. My first holiday was when I was about two and we went to Malta. Then we went to Spain and France, and as we got older we went to DisneyWorld and Turkey. And we've got family in America so we went there a few times.

What's been your best holiday ever?

H: I went to Turkey with my friends. There are loads of bars and nightclubs and the biggest open air disco ever. It was fantastic.

Faye: Last year when I went to Greece. I did water-skiing and paragliding and everything.

Claire: I always love going to America because I'm a shopaholic!

Lee: I've had a few. Because I was a footballer I used to go on all the football trips with the school to Spain and that. I met Gary Lineker a few times and I went to the Barcelona stadium and stuff.

Lisa: My family took me to Hawaii which was amazingly beautiful. I want to go back there one day.

WHERE DID YOU GO ON YOUR FIRST HOLIDAY

AWAY FROM YOUR PARENTS?

Faye: I went to Gran Canaria with my boyfriend when I was 16. My boyfriend at the time had to go and ask my dad if I could go! It was an 18-30 holiday and we had such a laugh playing volleyball and going on banana boats.

H: When I was 13 I went to Canada touring with a play, and then when I was 18 I went to Turkey with my mates.

Lee: It was on the first football trip I went on. We had all these games set up against the Spanish teams – it was brilliant!

Lisa: I went to Majorca with my boyfriend when I was 17. I had a good time, but I still prefer going with my family and I'd go away with them tomorrow.

Claire: When I was about 18 I went to Tenerife with my friend Joanne. It wasn't very good because we had £200 spending money between us, and we stayed in a hotel that was full of families. Not much fun.

Have you ever worn embarrassing beach attire?

Lisa: I don't like the bikini I wore in "5,6,7,8." It's green and had little shorts – it was horrible!

Faye: Not really, I usually end up wearing a swimming costume with a T-shirt on top. But I remember my mum making me and my sister wear matching towelling shorts when we were younger!

Lee: I wear Speedo trunks to sunbathe in when I'm around the pool because I hate getting tan lines. But if I'm going in the sea, I put my shorts on.

Claire: I only ever wear a bikini, and you can't go wrong with that, can you?

H: Well I don't think they're embarrassing, but everyone seems to think that my Speedos aren't very nice. The band say they've got a saggy bum, but they haven't!

How much stuff do you take with you when you go on holiday?

Faye: Loads – I like to be equipped!

Claire: I used to take loads, but now I know better and I just take bikinis and a few things for the evenings.

Lee: I usually just take a case full. Enough to get me by.

Lisa: I take a lot, but because all my stuff is lycra it folds up really small so I can take a good selection.

H: When I was younger I used to take about three outfits per day, but these days I just take the essentials.

What beach games do you play?

Lee: Bat and ball and frisbee, and I love swingball although you don't often see that on the beach – it doesn't stick in the sand very well!

Faye: Volleyball, and I've tried frisbee but I'm such a girl I'm always worried about breaking my nails. I like sponge tennis as well, and that game where you have velcro pads and you have to throw a ball at them.

Lisa: I just like volleyball, I'm not into bat and ball or anything.

Claire: I like building sandcastles, although I'm not very good at it!

H: I like building sandcastles as well, especially ones with a big moat! I'm getting pretty good at them these days…

Are you a good sunbather?

Faye: I'm a sun worshipper!

Lisa: Me and Faye are the best. I can lie there for hours if I've got a book to read.

I LIKE TO WRITE IN MY DIARY AS WELL. I'VE KEPT A DIARY SINCE

DAY ONE OF STEPS – IT'LL BE WORTH SOMETHING ONE DAY!

Claire: I'm brilliant, but not quite as good as Faye and Lisa.

Lee: I'm brilliant as well! But I hate getting tan lines and you always get a white bum, so I sometimes go on a sunbed to even it out.

H: I'm not very good at all. I get really bored and fidget. It takes me half an hour to put my sun cream on, and by then I'm bored. I don't tan either, so I can't be bothered.

What's the best thing about holidays?

H: You get to chill out and eat melons on the beach.

Faye: The fact that you can put your mobile phone down and no-one can ring you. Just being able to get away and know that you can be impulsive and do what you want – you've got total freedom.

Lee: Getting away from England and doing something different. You can go out when you want, not have a care in the world, and get a tan!

Lisa: Getting a tan, I love having a tan!
Claire: Getting a tan is the only reason I go!

What do you like to do when you have time off?

Faye: Stay in my bed! But if it's nice weather outside I like to get out, and I love going to Greenwich market.

H: I like to see my friends and spend lots of money. I've also just joined the School of Meditation. I thought it would be all airy-fairy, but it's brilliant.

Claire: Absolutely nothing. Either stay at home or go shopping or go to the cinema. I'm really lazy so I like to slob around.

Lee: I like chilling out in my room watching a video, playing Playstation, or writing some music.

Lisa: I usually see my friends. I've got a lot of good friends so I make sure I see them all and party whenever I get a chance.

You've got the album, you love the single, now dance along with our Step by Step guide to...

Last Thing On My Mind

1 Make sure you're wearing your beach clothes! Now, turn to the right and roll your arms around each other.

2 Do the same on your left hand side. Repeat twice.

3 Jump to the left and bring your arms up by the side of you. Take two steps to your right.

4 Bring your arms up in front of your face.

5 Swing them out to the side with your thumbs aloft. Repeat steps four and five.

6

Put your right leg in front of your right. Throw your arms in the air in a V-shape pointing upwards.

7

Criss-cross your arms in front of you and point your right leg to the side. Repeat.

8

Face the front and bend your left leg. Place your left hand on your hip and raise your right hand in the air and point your finger!

9

Whirl your hands as though you're shampooing your hair and shake your booty as you turn around! Congratulations, looking a divvy on the dance floor is now the last thing on your mind!

IN BETWEEN DOMINATING THE CHARTS AND
TEACHING EVERYONE A WHOLE HOST OF NEW
DANCE ROUTINES, STEPS HAVE SOMEHOW FITTED IN
TIME TO TRAVEL THE WORLD!

Stepping Around The World

The countries!

Steps have done their fair share of globetrotting, notching up thousands of miles flying everywhere from Spain to South Africa.

While they've enjoyed every second of their romps around the world, the band can't help having their favourite countries. Faye loved visiting Australia, and she was stunned by the response they got out there. "Everyone knew us even though we'd never been there before. We'd had two number ones with '5, 6, 7, 8' and 'Last Thing On My Mind,' and everyone was so nice to us and such brilliant fun!"

Lisa feels the same, "I really liked Australia because it's quite English and there are lots of young people around. I could definitely live there, I felt really at home."

Lee's favourite place is Singapore because, just like him, it's incredibly neat! "It's so cleanly kept. You step off a plane and all these trees and bushes are perfectly pruned and there's no rubbish anywhere – it's amazing!"

Claire agrees with Faye, Lisa and Lee, and rates Australia and Singapore as her top destinations.

"But to be honest, I've loved most of the places we've visited. We've had some incredible experiences."

H, ON THE OTHER HAND, PREFERS SOMEWHERE A LITTLE CLOSER TO HOME.

"I love Cannes in the south of France. It's fantastic, there are loads of little restaurants everywhere and everyone's rollerblading and having fun. It's so laid back."

The glamour!

Although they've scored huge hits in all the countries they've visited, they still get freaked out by all the attention they attract when they go abroad – especially when they visit Taiwan. Claire recalls the first time they went. "We'd just arrived after a zillion-hour flight and we were absolutely knackered. When we pulled up at our hotel there were all these limousines in front us and loads of butlers and maids standing outside with flowers. I went, 'Guys, someone really important must have just arrived.'

"We all had our faces pressed up against the window of the bus, then the doors opened and we all just fell out…" A stunned H takes up the story, "And it was all for us! Can you believe that? The whole of the hotel had come out to greet us!"

Faye laughs and admits that they initially thought the welcome was for the president or something. "But it really was for us. And there we were, sprawled out on the floor, dishevelled in our hats and sunglasses!"

And it didn't stop there. While they were doing a mall gig, they had a whopping sixty bodyguards looking after them, and fans passing out all around them. Lee was stunned. "There were thousands of fans, and some of them were fainting and being carried out. I was thinking, 'This is mad, it's just us on stage and all this mayhem's going on.' It was shocking. It was the first time I'd experienced anything like that.

"They were treated like royalty everywhere they went. "The bodyguards would stop traffic so we could cross the road, and we had a 24-hour butler service in our hotel. It was totally unnecessary, but we weren't complaining," H laughs.

The food!

It may all sound like something out of a Hollywood movie, but trotting around the world isn't all glamour – they've had to sample some pretty revolting grub along the way!

FAYE WAS HORRIFIED WHEN SHE AND LISA TRIED OYSTERS IN FRANCE, AND DISCOVERED THAT THEY'RE STILL ALIVE WHEN YOU EAT THEM!

Lisa was still brave enough to try snails after her traumatic experience, but you won't be surprised to hear that Faye turned down the offer of octopus!

But Lee doesn't mind a bit of experimentation with his chow, and even ate a real cow's tongue in Hong Kong. He also admits to chomping on octopus eggs which he reckons were 'quite nice'!

H is like Lee, and is willing to try anything – as long as he can manage to eat it! "In the Philippines it's not polite to use a knife and fork, so when we ordered pork we had to eat it with our fingers. They literally brought out a whole pig with a thick fat skin and we had to try and pick bits off. It was funny."

But while H and Lee will try anything, Claire is a bit more picky about her nosh. "I won't eat odd food, but one time we went to this place in Japan where we were filming this TV show and we all had to try these desserts.

"There was this black jelly stuff that didn't taste of anything, and these other puddings that looked like blown up pictures of cells! I only tried them because I knew they wouldn't contain anything too weird like strange meat. But I still wasn't sure what I was eating."

Eurgh!

The fans!

Steps have met some brilliant people on their travels, and a fair sprinkling of bananas fans! Lee says that although the fans in Hong Kong are lovely, they do have a funny habit. "They'll run up and scream in your face, then five minutes later they'll do it again!"

"And sometimes they throw themselves on stage while you're performing." Claire says looking worried.

"In Singapore they actually ask you if they can scream at you, though." Faye continues, "They come right up to you and say 'Can we do this?' and scream in your face! Then they carry on screaming!"

They also get pretty excitable in the Philippines. "At one point we had to run away from all these fans – it was like a stampede!" H laughs.

But there are also plus points to having enthusiastic fans – presents! Lee gets given everything from Tommy Hilfiger jackets to watches, the girls get jewellery and drawings, while H gets toys! But the most bizarre present award has to go to Claire. "I got given two sewing kits on one trip!" she giggles. "I don't know why, because I've never even said I liked them!"

Strange goings on!

Of course, with different countries come different traditions, and Steps have come across a few of the most interesting ones imaginable. Lee thinks it's bizarre that "in some south-east Asian countries you're not allowed to chew chewing gum. You can actually get done for it." Faye was a bit shocked when she went out to dinner in one exotic country. "I can't remember where we were, but we were having dinner, and at the end of the meal everyone started belching at each other. Apparently it's the polite thing to do if you've enjoyed your meal, but I found it very strange and a bit rude. It's alright if you're out with your mates, but not with people you don't know!"

CLAIRE DOESN'T LIKE THE FACT
THAT YOU HAVE TO TAKE YOUR SHOES
OFF IN LOADS
OF PLACES IN
HONG KONG.

"We went to this radio station where unless you wore these special slippers, you weren't allowed to walk in certain places!"

As for H's strangest experience abroad? Well it may not be a tradition, but it could become a regular thing unless he's careful. "I was winding the band up when we were in Sweden so they stripped me and locked me outside starkers. I had to grab a tea towel to hide my bits and pray that no-one saw me while I begged to be let back in!"

Scary stuff!

Steps have also had more than their fair share of natural disasters on their travels. They encountered an earthquake in Japan, and far from being scared, Faye found it quite exciting! "It's the best feeling in the world. Imagine a huge thunderstorm and times it by a million. The whole room was moving beneath our feet. It was like being on a huge funfair!"

Shortly afterwards they also got "ashed on" in Japan: "It rained, bringing all this volcano ash down with it. We were walking along and suddenly our clothes were black!" says Lisa.

"We couldn't believe it!" exclaims Claire, "The whole area was reduced to rubble and loads of trees were knocked down. Luckily we managed to persuade the count of another mansion nearby to let us film there."

Then there was the tornado in Italy which was so fierce it totally wiped out the location they were planning to use for "One For Sorrow".

AND FINALLY THERE WAS

THE MONSOON IN

BANGKOK.

It was so severe that the water reached up past the doors of the van the band were travelling in. "We couldn't open the doors or anything, we'd have got totally soaked. It was scary." Lee says.

Blimey, remember never to go on holiday with Steps!

Shopping around the globe!

It won't come as any surprise to hear that when it comes to shopping, the girls in the band are the experts. Lisa loves picking up anything cute and unusual, and scouring the clothes shops. Faye loves picking up mobile phone gadgets, and rates a miniature leather camel as her favourite thing she's bought abroad. Claire considers her mini Polaroid camera as her best buy, and loves searching out bargain clothes.

As for the boys, the only thing Lee buys is duty-free aftershave, while H likes picking up the odd gadget. He once bought a fantastic watch in Singapore, and is gutted about the fact that he lost it. "I loved that watch. When you went through different time zones you could just touch a button and it changed for you. And it automatically changed when it was a leap year. I want it back," he sniffs.

America is next for the Steps treatment. The band already have an American agent and have visited the US to show everyone what the band are all about. They've also been doing a lot of work in South Africa, and are continuing to visit all the places where they've already secured success.

Lee

When were you born?

28th January 1975

Where were you born?

Chester

What time?

5.25am. My sister was born at exactly the same time as me but in the evening.

What's the naughtiest thing you did at school?

Probably breaking a window. I had a habit of doing that whenever I was playing football.

What was the first item of clothing you bought?

I bought some jeans with patches on from my local market.

What was your favourite/least favourite subject at school?

I really liked CDT because I got to make things like video cabinets, but I didn't like anything boring!

Who was your best friend at school?

I didn't have one particular friend, I just had the gang that hung around Seymour Drive where I lived. A guy called Simon Grisdale became a good friend from 14 onwards, though.

Where did you used to hang out with your mates?

On the football field having a kick around. Also, my parents used to let me and my friends have the house to ourselves every Saturday night. They'd go out for a drink and they'd put bin bags around for rubbish, and let us watch videos and stuff.

What was your first taste of showbiz?

I played King Herod in the Nativity Play when I was in infant school. I remember coming home crying to my mum because I didn't want to be King Herod because he killed Jesus!

Who was the first celebrity you met?

I went to a roadshow once where Danni Minogue was performing. It was live on air so we had to be dead quiet, and I waited until it was silent and then I jumped up and shouted "Daaaaniiii!" She blew me a kiss and waved, so I sort of met her.

Have you got anything pierced?

I've got nothing pieced, and no tattoos!

What was the first record you bought?

There were two. "Karma Chameleon" by Culture Club and "Pass The Dutchie" by Musical Youth.

What about your first celebrity crush?

Helena Christiansen.

What did you want to be when you were young?

A footballer.

What colour is your bath towel at home?

I've got loads: blue, multi-coloured, striped… You name it!

What's your duvet like?

I've got two – a blue and white striped one, and a tartan one.

What's your favourite TV programme?

Friends.

What's your favourite kind of fish?

I don't really like fish, so I'll say cod because it's easy to eat.

What's your favourite flower?

Roses.

What's the most expensive thing you've ever bought?

My first car, although my parents and grandparents helped me out with it.

What's your biggest regret?

Not pushing myself enough when I was younger. I think I missed out on things because of it.

What's your biggest triumph?

Steps! I always said I wanted to leave my name in the world in some way, and now I'm going to.

What makes you laugh until you cry?

Funny movies, or someone tickling me!

Who was the last person you fancied?

The actress Salma Hayek.

What's the weirdest rumour you've heard about yourself?

When Steps first started this magazine said that I was quitting to go solo. I hadn't even done an interview with them!

How long do you take to get ready?

It depends where I'm going, but I'm pretty quick. I can be ready in 10-15 minutes.

Who's your favourite Disney character?

Aladdin.

What do you always carry around in your bag?

Whatever I need, hahaha! But I've always got my phone.

How do you have your tea?

Milk and one sugar.

How much sleep do you need?

Eight hours is ample for me.

What can't you live without?

The love and respect of my family.

Have you got a special teddy?

No, but I've got some *South Park* toys. I've got a great one where Kenny's head gets ripped off!

What do you hope no-one ever finds out?

There's nothing really. Although I don't like people invading my personal family space.

Tell us a secret!

I'm really only six, and I've got a habit of eating cereal before I go to bed.

Steps And Santa

What's been your best Christmas ever?

H: Last year. I had a bit of money so I treated all my friends and family.

Lee: when I was younger I got a BMX bike, and the helmet and gloves and everything. I was out doing wheelies all day!

Faye: I remember getting my first pair of roller skates and being so pleased. They were white with red wheels.

Claire: Probably one when I was a kid. Christmas is so exciting when you're young.

Lisa: Last year when we'd got to number one – it was a double celebration.

When do you start getting excited about Christmas?

Lee: As soon as my advent calendar opens, that's it.

Claire: As soon as the tree goes up 12 days before Christmas. Last year was the first year that I didn't try to peek at my presents!

H: I'm always excited! when Christmas is over I start getting excited for the next one!

Lisa: On Faye's birthday in November because I know it means that Christmas is nearly here!

Faye: Same here!

What's your favourite thing about Christmas?

Lisa: Seeing my family is the best thing because we don't always get a chance.

Faye: Crackers. You always get some really useless presents and I nick everyone else's. I love getting those fortune teller fish.

Lee: Everything! Everyone changes and there's a nice atmosphere everywhere.

H: Terry's Chocolate Orange and *The Wizard of Oz*.

Claire: Presents, that's all Christmas is for! No, Christmas is a time for loving and giving and… presents!

IS THERE ANYTHING YOU DON'T LIKE

ABOUT

CHRISTMAS?

Claire: It's really boring when everyone falls asleep after dinner. And there are no presents left!

Faye: Boxing Day. You know that it's turkey again and the TV's not as good. And you have to kiss loads of hairy-lipped aunties!

Lee: Probably the overratedness of it. It should be about family.

Lisa: Where I live it's snows quite a lot so I get really disappointed when it doesn't and I can't go tobogganing.

H: My mum's gravy, but don't tell her!

When did you stop believing in Santa?

H: What do you mean? He's a real person!

Faye: I was quite young. I'm a light sleeper and I caught my dad putting the presents out.

Lee: I found out through friends when I was quite young. I hid it from my sister for a long time afterwards, though.

Lisa: It just happened, and I was really sad when it did.

Claire: I can't remember, but I still put out mince pies and stuff until a few years ago. I love the idea of Santa.

What's the best present you've ever been given?

Faye: My roller boots, and my first ever locket. I felt so grown up and ladylike when I got my first piece of jewellery.

Claire: Last year I got a brand new double bed. It's so nice.

Lee: I got a bike called a Speedway. There was a knock at the door and everyone said, 'Go and see who it is, it might be Santa!' And when I opened the door this bike was sitting there!

Lisa: A working dolls house with lights and doors and curtains. It was absolutely beautiful, but it got broken. I was gutted.

H: We all got given a big caricature picture of ourselves last year, they were brilliant.

What's the worst present you've ever been given?

Lisa: I can't say because I'll feel awful! At the end of the day it's a present and that's fine.

Lee: One year my grandparents gave me and my dad matching jumpers. They were brown with darker brown spots on them.

Faye: A bag of cotton wool balls and slippers. They were nasty moccasin slippers.

H: Plastic cockroaches that some fans gave me!

CLAIRE: I ALWAYS GET GIVEN TIGHTS BY MY MUM. I HAVEN'T WORN TIGHTS SINCE I WAS AT SCHOOL!

What's the best present you've ever given someone?

Faye: I was going away so I gave a friend a plane ticket so they could come and visit me.

Claire: I got my sister loads of clothes last year, and she was really grateful. I love buying people nice things.

Lee: I gave my mum and dad a platinum disc last year. My mum started crying, it was really lovely.

Lisa: I took my family to Tenerife on holiday last year. It was so rewarding to be able to do it.

H: I bought my parents a holiday to Lanzarote. I loved doing that.

What's the dodgiest present you've ever given someone?

H: I bought my friend a blow-up sheep and he wasn't amused!

Faye: It's shocking, but you know when you get a nasty present the year before and you… um, give it to someone the next year? I did that.

Lisa: I've done the same thing I'm afraid!

Claire: Nothing too bad, but I'm terrible at buying presents.

Lee: Nothing! Forgetting to buy someone something is the worst thing.

What would be your ideal Christmas?

Faye: Snow on Christmas day, far too many presents, all your mates round, and being able to watch whatever TV you wanted.

Lisa: As long as my family are there and I've got enough money to buy them something nice, I'm happy.

Claire: I'd like to try going abroad and spending it on a beach.

Lee: I'd like to take my close friends and family away somewhere where it's snowing, to a little log cabin or something.

H: The Wizard Of Oz, Baileys, Chocolate Orange, my friends and family, and I'm happy.

You've got the album, you love the single, now dance along with our Step by Step guide to...

One For Sorrow

1

Place your left hand inside your right elbow and pump arm backwards twice.

2

Place your right hand inside your left elbow and pump arm backwards twice.

Girls: Place your right then left hand on the back of your head.

3

4

Boys: Pump both arms together twice.

5

Make a quarter turn and clap hands at waist level behind...

... and then in front of you.

6

7

Point right hand straight up with your forefinger making a 'one'.

Bring your middle finger up to make a 'two'.

8

Bring your fingers down to eye level.

9

Sweep your fingers over your eyes like a mask. Superb! Now you won't look a sorry sight down the disco!

10

WHAT CAN THEY COOK? WHAT WOULD THEY NEVER EAT? AND WHO WOULD THEY MOST LIKE TO HAVE LUNCH WITH? READ ON AND FIND OUT...

5,6,7, EAT!

What are your favourite foods?
Faye: I know it sounds really boring but I really like salads. I'm a real celery freak, and I like spreading soft cheese in the middle – it's delicious!
H: Everything and anything, but I especially love lobster.
Lisa: I love chicken, pasta and spaghetti bolognese.
Claire: I like cheeseburgers and junk food. I'd live on takeaways if I could!
Lee: Spaghetti bolognese.

What do you dislike?
Lisa: I don't like avocado or oysters. I like simple, traditional food.
Claire: Fish, or spicy foods. I can't eat things like veal or pigeon either. Eurgh!
H: Anything spicy.
Faye: Mushy peas, hummus, mashed potato – in fact, anything mashed.
Lee: Prunes, and I'm not a big fish lover.

What would you never try?
Claire: Things like monkey's brains or sheep's eyes. How disgusting!
Lee: Sushi looks horrible.
Faye: I'd never eat weird meat. My sister went to South Africa and she tried elephant and giraffe meat.
H: I'll try anything once! I wouldn't eat oysters though. I tried them once and they were disgusting.
Lisa: Monkey brains. They eat them in Asia.

What do you eat when you're on the road?

Lisa: I eat a lot of pot noodles because they're easy!

Lee: We have a lot of service station sandwiches. Or fast food from a burger place.

Faye: It's usually a sandwich, a packet of crisps and a bar of chocolate.

H: In the beginning we'd just have pasties and stuff, but we do eat better now.

Claire: On the last tour we had meals cooked for us every night which was brilliant.

ARE YOU A HEALTHY EATER?

CLAIRE: NOPE!

Lisa: I am, but I treat myself every now and again. I work out so I'm allowed to!

H: You've got to stay healthy because if you get run down and ill you can't work.

Faye: I do things in moderation. I do love healthy food, but I love junk food as well.

Lee: I am, yes. I eat loads of fruit, pasta, chicken, cereal and grapefruit – I'm pretty good!

Do you eat a lot of junk food?

Claire: Loads of it!

Lisa: Claire eats enough for the whole band! But I only eat it rarely.

Faye: I do eat it, but if I've eaten too much junk food and I'm starting to feel wobbly round the edges I'll go back to eating healthily again.

Lee: Sometimes if I'm in a rush I'll grab something like a burger.

H: I like junk food, but everything in moderation!

What are your favourite sweets?

Faye: I like eclairs; I also like anything mint chocolate, and candy nuts are lovely.

Lisa: I love flumps, they're gorgeous.

H: Jelly eggs, mmmmmm! And milk bottles and fizzy cola bottles.

Lee: I don't eat a lot of sweets, but I love ice-cream and banana milkshakes.

Claire: Those fizzy red lace things and popping candy. I used to buy ten packets at a time!

Are you a whizz in the kitchen?

Faye: That's somewhere you'll never find me!

Claire: I can get by, but it takes me ages to make anything.

Lee: I'm not a whizz, but I know how to cook what I like. I can cook chicken curry, spaghetti bolognese, lasagne, pies – that sort of thing.

H: Not at all. Whenever anyone comes round I make them a jacket potato with something in it!

Lisa: I'm quite good when I get the chance and my speciality is chilli con carne. Me and my brother Anthony used to make lovely chocolate chip and cherry cookies as well.

What's the most adventurous thing you can cook?

H: Jacket potatoes, but I can do them with cheese, beans, ketchup – you name it! I made spaghetti bolognese once but it wasn't very nice. Claire's a good cook, though.

Claire: I made Lobster Thermidor once, and I've made tomato, leek and onion soup. I used to make cakes a lot as well. They were pretty good!

Lisa: I cooked chicken paella once and it actually turned out really well.

Faye: Fried egg sandwiches and toasties. I can do all sorts of toasties actually! Cheese, ham, anything… And I'm good at cooking salads!

Lee: Lasagne. It's quite easy to make but it does take bit of thought.

Who would you most like to have lunch with?

Faye: Madonna. Wouldn't that be interesting? She's so clever and I'm so inspired by her. Let's do lunch, Madge!

Lisa: I'm the same as Faye, I think Madonna would be brilliant!

Lee: George Michael. He's amazing and I'd love to have a really good chat with him about his life. I think he's incredibly interesting.

H: If it could be anyone, it would be Marilyn Monroe. She was incredible.

Claire: Prince, but I'm not sure whether he'd talk! He might just sit there and not say anything, and I'd be really disappointed. Maybe I could go to the cinema with him instead?

Faye

When were you born?

14th November 1975

Where were you born?

Northampton

What time?

5.30am

What's the naughtiest thing you did at school?

When I was seven I got caught in the junior toilets with my back against one cubicle wall, and my legs against the other, and I was climbing up to the top. The headmistress made me and my friends clean the toilet walls down!

What was the first item of clothing you bought?

A pair of jeans when I was about 14.

What was your favourite/least favourite subject at school?

I didn't like History and Geography, but I really liked art and drama.

Who was your best friend?

I started school a year early, so I had to be kept down a year when I was eight. So until then my best friend was Jenny Swain, then when I changed years it was Lisa Valentine.

Where did you used to hang out with your mates?

Anywhere I could get away with!

What was your first taste of showbiz?

When I was six I did my first ever song and dance. I sang Michael Jackson's "Ben" to a bunny rabbit on stage!

Who was the first celebrity you met?

Davy Jones (singer from massive 60s band The Monkees) when I did my first pantomime when I was six. He was really sweet and he gave us all Christmas presents of some bubble bath, a picture of a cat and a signed photo of him.

When did you get your ears pierced?

When I was 16. I wasn't allowed until then, so then I got three, and my belly button pierced!

What was the first record you bought?

I can't remember, but I know it was something dodgy!

Who was your first crush on?

Adam Ant. He was gorgeous.

What did you want to be when you were young?

A dancer, I wanted to be a prima ballerina or something. But I was told I wasn't the right shape to be a ballerina.

What colour's your bath towel at home?

Yellow.

What's your duvet like?

I've just bought a new one, and it's a nice white cotton one.

What's your favourite TV programme?

Jerry Springer. If you've got cable you can watch him about six times a day!

What's your favourite kind of fish?

I'm a big tiger prawn freak.

What's your favourite flower?

Sunflowers.

What's the most expensive thing you've ever brought?

I bought a three-pronged 1920s lamp that's been re-covered in cow print fabric. It's brilliant but it cost a lot.

What's your biggest regret?

Stopping playing the saxophone. I can't play it anymore because I've got a minor form of lockjaw.

What's your biggest triumph?

I didn't ever think I'd be a pop person so getting to number one was amazing. I'm so proud.

What makes you laugh until you cry?

There's a scene in Flubber where this stuff explodes and this ball goes flying round this house and hits everything. I had to rewind it about six times and I was crying laughing!

Who was the last person you fancied?

I used to fancy Leonardo DiCaprio, but now I quite like the boys in Westlife – I think they've got great potential!

What's the weirdest rumour you've heard about yourself?

That I once re-enacted the scene with the clay from Ghost. It was ridiculous! Also according to the papers one week I was dating a Belgium rock star, and the next week I was dating a Dutch drummer!

How long do you take to get ready?

About an hour if I'm doing a full whack routine.

Who's your favourite Disney character?

Tasmanian Devil.

What do you always carry around in your bag?

Lip balm, mascara, purse, phone and sunglasses.

How do you have your tea?

White with one sugar.

How much sleep do you need?

Six hours and I'm fresh.

What can't you live without?

The sunshine – it really depresses me when we have loads of really dark days.

Have you got a special teddy?

I didn't have one because I gave them all to a children's home when I moved out of my parents house. But then I bought one recently. It's this massive floppy dog with massive ears, and it's got sand in its feet so you can make it cuddle you!

What do you hope no-one ever finds out?

I can't say because then everyone will know! I used to think it would be really bad if anyone found out I wasn't a natural blonde, but now I quite like being plastic, hahaha!

Tell us a secret!

I've got a bit of a shoe fetish for mules! I've got 14 pairs and I hardly ever wear them because they're not very comfortable.

THEY'VE LAUGHED AND THEY'VE NEARLY CRIED AS THEY'VE FILMED THEIR SIX STUPENDOUS VIDEOS. READ ON FOR TALES OF WEDDINGS, INJURED BOTTOMS AND GIANT INSECTS!

Video Stars!

5, 6, 7, 8

Steps flew to Malaga in Spain and threw a beach party for their very first video. While they were all dead excited, everyone had a touch of nerves and didn't know what to expect. The girls were all the more anxious because they had to wear skimpy bikinis whilst dancing on sand and being told to sing sexily at the camera. "The director kept saying, 'Look sexy darling' but I felt ridiculous!" laughs Faye. "We didn't eat much lunch on the day of the shoot because we wanted our tummies to look flat. We gorged the night after, though!"

And it wasn't just the band that gorged. There were swarms of insects keen to nibble on the Steps' girls bodies – especially Claire's legs! "I got bitten to death, I had these huge bites all over my legs."

As if that wasn't enough to contend with, the girls also had the hairdresser from hell. Not only did she back-comb Claire's hair into a bouffant, but she made such a mess of Lisa's that she ended up hiding from the hairdresser in the toilets. "She was Spanish and they have a very different way of doing hair over there. She gave me this terrible quiff so I brushed it out and hid from her until we had to start filming. I kept hearing her going, Liiiiisaaaa, Liiiiisaaaa, I must do your hair.' And I thought, 'No chance!'"

But the boys had no complaints. Lee relished every minute of his debut performance, especially as the entire beach got closed off for the filming and he got to do his solo rap. "I'd love to go into films one day, so getting a chance to do a bit of rapping on my own was great. I felt like I was in a movie."

H says he got over-excited by the smallest thing, and even went to the gym to make sure he looked his best. "I'm never going to be a sex god, but I wanted to look good!" he says.

Last Thing on My Mind

Fantastic Cuba was the destination for the "Last Thing On My Mind" video. But while they had the time of their lives, there are two sides to every story, as H tells us. "The villa we used over there was beautiful, but there was so much poverty in the old town. It was good to see the real side and it really opened our eyes, but I found it a bit depressing and I was quite upset." Claire agrees, "It's so shocking when you see things like that in a country so beautiful. It really brings things home to you."

They spent a week in Cuba, giving them a chance not only to film the video, but also to do a spot of sunbathing and partying! "All the extras were brilliant and we partied hard after filming had finished." Faye recalls with a smile. "We learnt loads of Cuban songs and hung out on the beach singing and dancing. It was wicked!" continues H.

"We had the best laugh doing this video," Lee agrees. "I got to drive around in a big car and hang out by the pool and party. It's hardly work, is it?"

One For Sorrow

"One For Sorrow" was filmed in beautiful Italy, and the Stepsters flew in from all over the world after having a week off. Claire arrived first as she had the most to film, and was shocked to discover that their location had been wiped out by a tornado. Luckily they swiftly found a new location – a huge villa near Lake Garda – and set to work.

The grass was green, the sun was shining, but little did video-viewers know that directly opposite where Steps were filming was, er, a sewage plant. But the hideous smell wasn't the only annoying thing, as Claire tells us: "There were bugs everywhere and we kept wanting to swat them while we were dancing, but we had to carry on and smile though it," And smile they all did, even though poor Lisa felt like crying. "I put my hand in the air when we were doing the dance routine and I got bitten in my armpit. It was so painful I had tears in my eyes," she recalls.

Faye didn't escape the nightmare bugs either. She cringes as she remembers walking through the field full of long grass. "All these bugs kept flying up my skirt. I was trying to walk sexily and look sympathetically at Claire, but I had these huge grasshoppers up my skirt!"

Despite all the goings on, the gang still enjoyed their third video and were looking forward to filming their fourth, their first studio shoot.

Heartbeat

"I looked an idiot in this, I had to be rescued by the girls!" H smiles as he talks about their Christmas extravaganza. But jokes aside, all five Steps members loved making this video as they had a big hand in creating it. As well as coming up with the story idea themselves, they got to design their costumes and have a laugh in the process.

The girls were relieved about the fact that for once they didn't have to worry about the sun melting their make-up – although they did have the Skidoos and the skiing to contend with.

Claire freaked when she saw the massive platform the Skidoo was resting on. "I'm scared of heights and I was like, 'I can't get up there!' Eventually two people had to help me up and my knuckles were white where I was holding on so tightly!"

Faye's experience wasn't quite so scary, just a bit unnerving. "I'd never skied before so I had to have a proper instructor there and everything.

I was standing on a table with a wind machine blowing in my face. I was crying with laughter because I felt so ridiculous!"

The party scene at the end was the highlight for the band and they had a laugh having their own personal Christmas, and Faye loved all the confetti! "We all had our own props and I got to keep all the confetti." Surely Christmas is a time for giving?

Tragedy

"Tragedy" is without a doubt the band's favourite video, and they all rate the day as one of the best they've ever had. The biggest buzz for them was having all their friends and family in it, and having a chance to walk down the aisle dressed up in posh clothes.

"ALL OUR PARENTS WERE CRYING SO IT WAS LIKE A REAL WEDDING. EVERYONE LOVES A WEDDING!" SAYS H.

"We had such a good time filming it, it was always a dream of ours to get our mates and our families in a video because they're the most important people in the world to us."

Claire rates her pretend wedding as a very bizarre experience. "My dad had hold of my arm and my sister was walking behind me like a real wedding. It was surreal!" she says.

Meanwhile, Faye had a total false eyelash nightmare, "My beaded tiara kept getting stuck in my eyelashes and I had to keep re-shooting my scenes!"

But beautiful bride Lisa had an altogether more embarrassing experience. "Me and my dad had to go round the block in the wedding car about ten times during filming, and all these old ladies we kept passing at the bus stop obviously thought I'd been stood up. They were gossiping and looking at me really sympathetically. In the end I kept hiding every time we passed them!"

Lee's favourite thing about the video was the quirky storyline, while Faye reckons that the best thing is that wherever they are in the world, if the see the video on MTV, then the band get to see their parents! Aaahhhh!

Better Best Forgotten

This was another video shot in a studio, and the band describe it as the weirdest they've made so far. "It was quite fun to do," says Lee, "but we were making a lot of it up as we were going along, so it was quite strange. But I did like having the opportunity to do a bit of ad-libbing – it made things exciting."

Claire liked the fact that she got a lot of spare time in between takes to chat to her friends on the phone, although she feels terrible that she was too busy chatting to realise that Faye had had an accident. "I heard this big crash but I just thought the caterers had dropped something upstairs. I felt awful when I found out what had happened."

In fact, a glass wall had fallen down while Faye was filming a scene and sprayed splinters of glass everywhere. Faye laughs at the memory now, but she didn't see the funny side when she was lying on a bed surrounded by paramedics. "I didn't actually get hurt by the wall, but I got loads of glass splinters in my bum! I had to lie down while someone shone a torch on my bottom and the paramedics picked out all these splinters with tweezers! How embarrassing."

"All the crew members kept coming up and laughing at me. I was totally cringing!" Sounds like the video lived up to its title for Faye!

H thought it was a fun video, although he's not sure that everyone understood it. "It had a very British sense of humour and some weird bits so I don't think everyone got it!" he laughs.

As it was their last video from *Step One* everyone felt a bit strange when filming finished. As Lisa explains, "It was odd because we knew it was going to be the last video off the first album, so it was like the end of a chapter. It was the end of the beginning, if you know what I mean. But there are plenty more videos to come!"

Hurrah!

STEPS' PERFECT VIDEO!

Who would you most like to appear in a Steps video?

H: Tom Jones would be brilliant. Can you imagine?

Faye: I wouldn't mind if Leonardo DiCaprio came along. In fact, he could have played my husband in "Tragedy"!

Lisa: I'm totally into George Michael at the moment. I think he's amazing and I really respect him.

Lee: I'd love Madonna to be in one, she'd be incredible.

Claire: I'd love to get a load of other pop groups in one, and I think Robbie Williams would be cool.

Where would be your dream video location?

Lee: The MGM studios in L.A. We could use all the equipment and do loads of stunts!

Faye: Hawaii so I get a free holiday. They could film us having a party on the beach!

H: DisneyWorld without a doubt.

Lisa: I'm with H on that one, it would be such a laugh!

Claire: I'd like to go to a really exotic location with white sand and clear seas. Perfect!

You've got the album, you love the single, now dance along with our Step by Step guide to...

Tragedy

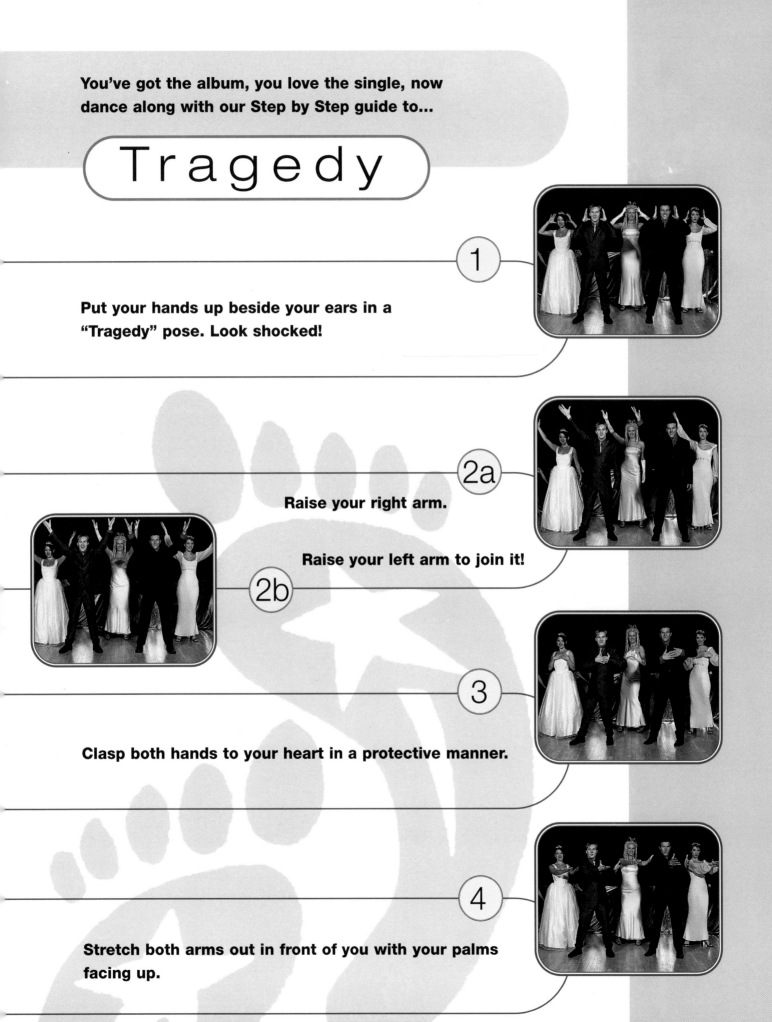

1

Put your hands up beside your ears in a "Tragedy" pose. Look shocked!

2a

Raise your right arm.

2b

Raise your left arm to join it!

3

Clasp both hands to your heart in a protective manner.

4

Stretch both arms out in front of you with your palms facing up.

Put your arms up to your head as in Step 1 and take a step to your right. Repeat the same move to your left, then repeat both moves again.

5a 5b

Place your right hand on your hip and step to the left, swinging your right arm out.
Repeat the same move to your right.

6a 6b

Hold your right arm out in a stopping traffic stylee!

7

Turn to your right and roll your left shoulder three times.
Brilliant! You definitely won't look tragic in front of your mates!

8

THEY'VE ALREADY COMPLETED A MASSIVELY SUCCESSFUL THEATRE TOUR, AND NOW THEY'RE READY TO TAKE ON THE BIG ARENAS. LET'S TAKE TO THE ROAD WITH STEPS!

This Band Will Tour Again!
Steps Live

What's was the best thing about doing your own tour?

Claire: Actually doing it! We'd spent so long talking about it and we've finally done it. It's what we've been aiming towards and it's made it all worth it.

H: We'd spent so much time doing other people's shows that it was brilliant getting to headline our own.

Lisa: I was in my element travelling and performing. Getting to sing live is really important to us because we are all singers.

Faye: It was brilliant singing live. We spend so much time talking about what we do, so it's so good to get on the microphone and sing live again. It's nice to quash the rumours that everyone in pop can't sing and get out there and give it some welly!

Lee: The best thing was that it was ours, in the fact that we had most of the control over it. We designed our own costumes and everything.

How long did it take you to rehearse for the shows?

Faye: We planned for about three months, but the actual rehearsals didn't take that long.

Claire: No, they took about three weeks in all. We knew all the dance routines already so we just had to stage it all and put movements to the slow songs. But I never know what to say on the in-between bits, so I was practising that!

DOES TOURING GET TIRING?

Lee: It does. If you could do it all in one place you'd be fine, but it's the travelling that tires you out. But you do get to chill out on the coach and you can play games and watch videos and stuff.

Lisa: But I could have gone on for another six months – I loved it so much!

H: It is brilliant, but it can be tiring when you have to do loads of interviews during the day when you've had a late night.

Claire: You have to look after yourself. It's so easy to party every night and burn yourself out, but I was a good girl and I made sure I got enough sleep!

Which song was most fun to perform?

Lee: A few for different reasons. I'd liked doing "Hero" because it was mine and H's chance to prove that we could sing live. And I love doing "Tragedy" because everyone loves it. And if you make a mistake you can look out into the audience and copy them!

Lisa: I really enjoyed singing "Stay With Me", which is the ballad that me and Faye did. Because it's slow there was no dance routine, so we got to sit down and sing to the audience.

H: I loved "One For Sorrow" because there's one bit when we put the lights up and everyone joins in; I felt so proud. I like "Hero" as well.

Claire: I thought "5, 6, 7, 8" was really fun, although it was a bit too energetic for me! I also liked all the ones where we got to really sing properly.

Faye: We revamped "5, 6, 7, 8" and did a complete hoedown. We had such a laugh. It was great to be able to take the mickey out of ourselves doing it.

What's the atmosphere like backstage before you go on?

Lee: The best ever! The warm up acts have been on and they've got the audience going, and at the end of the day you know the audience are there to see you. They've got their banners and they're screaming, and it's so exciting to know you're going to face that.

Lisa: It's brilliant, we vibe each other up and it's really exciting.

HOW DO YOU PREPARE FOR GOING ON STAGE?

Claire: We have a bit of time to ourselves and do some vocal warm-ups. Then we watch the dancers doing their stretching exercises and copy them – though we don't really know what we're doing!

Faye: Then we all put our hands together and blow raspberries or something. You know how some people pray and stuff? Well we totally respect that, but we just make jokes and say, "you roooock!" or something else stupid. It's a bit of group bonding before we go on!

H: We say silly words depending on where we are, things like "Scooby Doo", or "Way-ay man!"

Do you get nervous before you hit the stage?

Lisa: I did in Rhyl because it was the first show and it was my home town.

Lee: No, if anything I'm raring to go! I'm the one that's geeing everyone up and getting excited.

Claire: I was petrified on the first one, but then I started getting more excited. I got nervous when my family or friends were there, but apart from that I was fine.

H: I'm the same, I get nervous when I know my friends and family are watching.

Faye: I do sometimes, but I think it's very healthy. It means that you're thinking about your performance and you want to do it to the best of your own ability.

How do you feel when you first get out on stage?

Lee: Incredible!

H: We're at our best on stage so it's the best feeling!

Lisa: It was an amazing feeling seeing all those people smiling at us and singing along – it's one of the best feelings in the world. I was gutted when we finished the tour and I can't wait for the Arena Tour!

Faye: It takes your breath away because everyone's screaming and you think "this is for us! People like us!" It's the most amazing feeling.

Claire: You get an instant buzz from the audience, they go mad. On the first night I nearly collapsed because it was such a shock.

Did you have any stage nightmares?

Lisa: Yes, in Rhyl when all my family and friends were there. I had a tube top on and it kept falling down. I was heartbroken because my dad was in the audience, and I didn't want to look unprofessional and keep yanking it up. So every time we turned round in a dance routine I was pulling it up!

Faye: I fell over my shoelace once when we were in Nottingham. I nearly hit the floor but I just stopped myself and pretended it was part of the dance routine! There's also this part where I have to stand up on a box and come through these swinging doors, and one day the box broke and I got my foot stuck. What a struggle!

Claire: I walked into a bit of scaffolding and whacked my hip bone one night. It hurt so much but H just cracked up laughing, so I did, and I had to try and carry on and sing. It was terrible, it was so painful!

H: I'd just got some new trousers that had this material crossed across the back of them. I was centre stage and I jumped forward and got my heel caught in the criss-cross and my trousers fell down in front of everybody!

Lee: I didn't fall over or anything. I was the lucky one!

Did you have any good after-show parties?

Lisa: Loads. Every night was a party – it was fantastic!

Faye: We had far too many! It was lovely because we had so many support acts and dancers and stuff, so there was always someone to party with.

Lee: We had a good one in Manchester in this lovely restaurant and all my family came – that was really nice.

IT WAS REALLY NICE TO BE ABLE TO SHARE

THE EXCITEMENT WITH THEM.

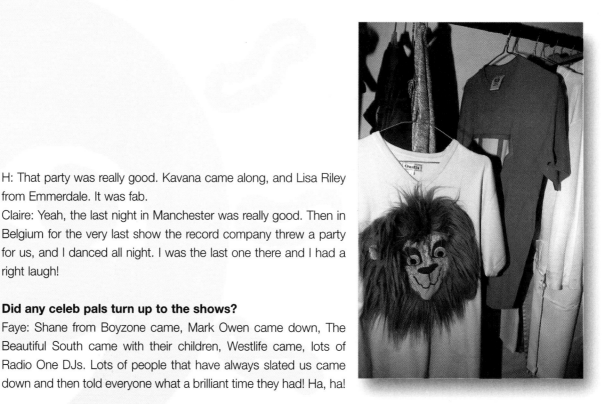

H: That party was really good. Kavana came along, and Lisa Riley from Emmerdale. It was fab.

Claire: Yeah, the last night in Manchester was really good. Then in Belgium for the very last show the record company threw a party for us, and I danced all night. I was the last one there and I had a right laugh!

Did any celeb pals turn up to the shows?

Faye: Shane from Boyzone came, Mark Owen came down, The Beautiful South came with their children, Westlife came, lots of Radio One DJs. Lots of people that have always slated us came down and then told everyone what a brilliant time they had! Ha, ha!

Did anyone play any practical jokes?

Lee: Yes, on the last night we grabbed hold of A1 and the girls covered them in glitter and make-up and we tied them up with sellotape and shoved them back on stage in front of everyone.

Faye: Lolly had some blow-up letters on stage and we pushed them over as well. We also bombarded Christian Fry with wet toilet roll bombs while he was performing.

H: But everyone was a good sport and they got us back!

Claire: During "Tragedy" balloons go out into the audience, and they covered them in shaving foam so it was everywhere!

Lisa: Us girlies used to have a giggle as well. We'd shout things at the male dancers and pinch their bums before they went on stage!

Sum up the tour?

H: The best thing ever, I want to do it all again now!

Lisa: Brilliant!

Lee: It's a total buzz from start to finish and I think it's what all bands work towards. Performing is what it's all about.

Claire: Totally, it was so important for us.

Faye: If I could I'd go on tour for life!

H

When were you born?

May 8th 1976

Where were you born?

Llwyniphia in the Rhondda, Wales.

What time?

Ooh, I don't know!

What's the naughtiest thing you did at school?

I did lots of naughty things at school, but the naughtiest thing I did was at home. We had this tank full of lovely fish like angel fish and tiger barbs, and I bought a terrapin and put it in the tank and it ate all the fish! My mum went up the wall.

What was the first item of clothing you bought?

I got a pair of checked jeans with Fred Flintstone on one leg and Barney Rubble on the other leg. Nice.

What was your favourite/least favourite subject at school?

I loved art, but I hated P.E. and having to play football. I once scored an own goal and I was so unpopular. Mind you, I liked swimming because I was a Welsh champion!

Who was your best friend?

I had lots, but my best friend now is called Billie and I've known her for about seven years.

Where did you used to hang out with your mates?

I was a member of an amateur theatre company so I used to go there a lot.

What was your first taste of showbiz?

I've been on the stage since I was nine, daaaarling!

Who was the first celebrity you met?

Max Boyce, a Welsh guy that used to sing with giant leeks. I met SuperTed when I was quite young as well.

When did you get your ears pierced?

I haven't, I don't like it.

What was the first record you bought?

Rick Astley's "Never Gonna Give You Up".

Who was your first celebrity crush on?

Tiffany and Debbie Gibson. Britney Spears is like the new Debbie Gibson!

What did you want to be when you were young?

A vet. My house was like a zoo. I had a tarantula called Boris, a dog called Ben, my fish – well, the ones my terrapin hadn't eaten – my terrapin, and a big lop-eared rabbit.

What colour's your bath towel at home?

Blue. I got it as a present when we went to the Philippines and it's got my name on it.

What's your duvet cover like?

I've just bought a checked Ralph Lauren one, it cost me a fortune!

What's your favourite TV programme?

Top Of The Pops.

What's your favourite kind of fish?

Cod.

What's your favourite flower?

Poppies. My gran passed away recently and they were her favourite flower, so whenever I see one it reminds me of her and makes my day better.

What's the most expensive thing you've ever bought?

I'm thinking about buying a house, so it's going to be that.

What's your biggest regret?

Giving up the guitar. If you play an instrument, keep at it!

What's your biggest triumph?

Getting to number one with "Tragedy". And our album launch as well – I cried on stage!

What makes you laugh until you cry?

Me and Lisa have a fantastic laugh, she has me in stitches. We'll be doing TV interviews and I'll pull faces at her when the camera's not on me and watch her squirm!

Who was the last person you fancied?

Britney Spears, although she's a bit young. I like Liv Tyler as well.

What's the weirdest rumour you've heard about yourself?

That I was a rampant redcoat! There were these pictures in the paper of me with all these girls that I supposedly snogged, but they were all my mates from back home!

How long do you take to get ready?

Ten minutes, quarter of an hour at the most.

Who's your favourite Disney character?

Simba from *The Lion King.*

What do you always carry around in your bag?

My phone, my diary, my snappy camera, my house keys, and I've started using a bum bag because I'm always losing my wallet.

How do you have your tea?

I like Earl Grey with milk and two sugars. But it has to be decaffeinated because caffeine makes me giddy!

How much sleep do you need?

I'd like to have a lot but I don't get the chance. But I can go for a few nights without sleep.

What can't you live without?

My friends, my family and my mobile phone.

Have you got a special teddy?

I've got a Forever Friends teddy that my friend gave me, and I've got a collection of frogs and Winnie the Pooh.

What do you hope no-one ever finds out?

I'm not telling you because then people will go and find out all about it!

Tell us a secret!

I want a puppy. A nice little companion.

Better Best Forgotten

FAYE ON LEE

ENGLISH

Have they got any favourite words?

"er...hello?!"

What's their best joke?

If it takes a man a week to walk a fortnight, how many beans in a barrel of grapes? (I didn't get it either!)

MATHS

What do they think is the biggest plus about being in Steps?

Seeing the world and doing what you enjoy.

How do they divide their time between the band and their normal life?

After work is over Lee spends time with his friends – seeing shows, going to the cinema and going to the gym – and on the phone to his family.

HISTORY

What's the naughtiest thing they've done in the past?

He's set up a pal on a blind date and there wasn't even a blind date involved! His pal thought he'd been stood up.

What's changed most about them since you first met?

His hair. (He parties a lot more nowadays too!)

DRAMA

What's the most outrageous thing they do?

He loves the feeling of danger – he's done a bungee jump and wants to jump out of a plane!

How much of a showoff are they?

He's a "right poser"!

BIOLOGY

What's their favourite part of their body?

His six-pack!

Who do they secretly fancy?

Jennifer Lopez.

H ON CLAIRE

ENGLISH

Have they got any favourite words?

"Cool!" And she shouts my name a lot to tell me to shut up!

What's their best joke?

Claire has really bad jokes. I like short punchlines, but hers go on for hours, so there's not enough paper to write one down!!

MATHS

What do they think is the biggest plus about being in Steps?

She gets to travel the world and do what she loves – singing.

How do they divide their time between the band and their normal life?

It's hard to divide time as we're always on the go, but Claire tries to involve her family and friends a lot by inviting them to gigs.

HISTORY

What's the naughtiest thing they've done in the past?

Claire makes mud pies out of the leftovers when we go out for a meal!

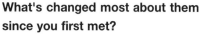

What's changed most about them since you first met?

She's a lot more confident now than when we first started. Claire used to get nervous a lot on stage – she still does now and again – but not as often.

DRAMA

How much of a showoff are they?

Claire's not a showoff at all. She likes performing on stage, but off stage Claire is like me – we'd rather put a baseball cap on and not get recognised.

BIOLOGY

What's their favourite part of their body?

I don't know.

Who do they secretly fancy?

Me! Claire usually likes her men dark, funny and good on the phone, but I'm not telling you who she fancies, it's a secret!

WHAT'S THEIR BEST JOKE?

LISA'S JOKES ARE USUALLY RUDE, SO I DON'T THINK YOU'LL BE

GETTING ANY OF THEM.

LEE ON LISA

ENGLISH

Have they got any favourite words?

Minger!

What's their best joke?

Lisa's jokes are usually rude, so I don't think you'll be getting any of them.

MATHS

What do they think is the biggest plus about being in Steps?

Sharing quality time with four good friends, seeing the world and becoming famous.

How do they divide their time between the band and their normal life?

Lisa loves the band, but partying will never leave her soul. (hence the name Party Steps)

HISTORY

What's the naughtiest thing they've done in the past?

Lisa has a problem of mooning out of car windows (I think it's the trousers she wears.)

What's changed most about them since you first met?

I think she's become more aware of herself and the way the music business works.

DRAMA

What's the most outrageous thing they do?

She uses every phone she finds.

How much of a showoff are they?

Lisa is a show off… BUT AREN'T WE ALL!

BIOLOGY

What's their favourite part of their body?

Her feet, because she always tiptoes!

Who do they secretly fancy?

Robbie Williams!

LISA ON H

ENGLISH

Have they got any favourite words?

'Food' and 'Are we there yet?'

What's their best joke?

What do you call a three legged donkey?
A wonkey! (Rubbish!)

MATHS

What do they think is the biggest plus about being in Steps?

Free food and clothes. Fan mail off girls.

How do they divide their time between the band and their normal life?

When H isn't working, he's sleeping!

HISTORY

What's the naughtiest thing they've done in the past?

There's so many! Probably the time he was under his bed and he lit a match and sang 'Happy Birthday to Me', then he set fire to his bed, which in turn set the whole house alight!!!

What's changed most about them since you first met?

He's more confident, but he does less sit-ups nowadays!

DRAMA

What's the most outrageous thing they do?

I love it when H bursts into song on the tube, or in the middle of the street – that really makes me laugh.

How much of a showoff are they?

H is the biggest showoff in the band, alongside me!

BIOLOGY

What's their favourite part of their body?

I don't think H has one. (He's got great legs though!)

WHO DO THEY SECRETLY FANCY?

ANYONE WHO FANCIES HIM!!!

CLAIRE ON FAYE

ENGLISH

What's their best joke?

I've never known Faye to tell any jokes. She was the only one who ever laughed at my tortoise joke. Because she found it funny I had to tell everyone we met, but no one else ever thought it was funny.

Have they got any favourite words?
Lush

MATHS

What do they think is the biggest plus about being in Steps?
Being able to travel all over the world!

How do they divide their time between the band and their normal life?
Faye has a good balance, she always

makes sure she has time for partying, decorating or doing her washing. Sometimes I don't know how she does it; if there is no time, she'll make it.

HISTORY

What's the naughtiest thing they've done in the past?
It's not really naughty, but Faye can stay up partying all night long and then go to work the next morning, I don't know how she does it.

What's changed most about them since you first met?
I wouldn't say that Faye has changed, she has a lot more knowledge about the business (as we all do) so she isn't afraid to open her mouth and say what she thinks.

DRAMA

What's the most outrageous thing they do?
Stay out all night partying!

How much of a showoff are they?
Faye is a huge showoff – she loves performing on stage.

BIOLOGY

What's their favourite part of their body?
Faye has got a great body. I would say her legs, but I don't know if she'd agree!

Who do they secretly fancy?
Faye did have a crush on Leonardo DiCaprio after she saw *Titanic*, but I think she's over him now.

You've got the album, you love the single, now dance along with our Step by Step guide to...

Better Best Forgotten

Bring your right hand up by the side of your face.

1

2

Do the same with your left hand your left hand.

3

Bring both arms down to shoulder level and face your palms outwards.

Bring your arms down lower and point your index fingers downwards.

4

Stay in position and point your fingers upwards.
Way-hey!
These moves won't be easily forgotten!

5

HOW COME STEPS ALWAYS LOOK SO GOOD? READ ON TO
FIND OUT THEIR SECRETS, AND DISCOVER THAT THEY DIDN'T
ALWAYS LOOK THIS COOL!

Steps Style!

Where do you buy your clothes?

Faye: Hype DF in Kensington. I also go to Oxford Street, and I get a lot of one-off things from abroad. I also get things made for me, which is great.

H: I think Top Man is really good, but I've got quite into my Gucci recently as well. I went to Harvey Nichols the other day and that was fantastic!

Lisa: I like places like Miss Selfridge, Top Shop and Jane Norman. I haven't been to Gucci and Armani yet; I don't like poncy stuff. I like fun, young stuff – and I love a bit of lycra!

Claire: I'll go anywhere, but specifically cheap places. I'd much rather get lots of cheap stuff than one thing that I'll only wear once.

Lee: I like to go to Selfridges because it's got everything under one roof. You can get Armani, Calvin Klein, Boxfresh – whatever you want.

Do you get any free?

Claire: Sometimes. We do design our own stuff and get it made these days which is cool. But that's stage stuff – I couldn't wear it out!

Lee: I've had some nice things from the fans; if anyone wants to give me anything, feel free! I like Armani by the way…

Faye: We get watches and stuff. The other day I got a letter from a guy who does body jewellery who asked if I wanted anything made. It's so exciting!

H: When you start out and you're skint you don't get anything, but now we're successful we're getting given things. Still, I'm not complaining!

Lisa: We did a photo shoot a while ago and I had this lovely top that's called a handkerchief top, and I said how much I liked it so I got sent one! I'll have to start saying I like more stuff now!

WHAT'S YOUR FAVOURITE ITEM

OF CLOTHING?

H: Any kind of hooded top – I live in them.

Faye: I've just bought a new pair of jeans that are the perfect fit.

Lee: I like funky jeans and smart baggy trousers, so anything I've got like that, really.

Lisa: I'm really into the trouser/skirt thing at the moment, I think it's really cute.

Claire: Trainers. I've got five different colours in one style, and I want some more!

What's the most money you've spent on one item of clothing?

Lee: A suit that I bought for the MTV awards which was about £290.

Faye: A pair of shoes for £250! They've got a straight plastic heel with a grey purply feather on the front. I've only worn them once, but I walk around the house in them because I love them so much!

H: I bought a leather jacket for £500 and I felt so bad that I phoned my dad and said, "Dad, I've done something really bad!"

Claire: I bought a full length winter coat for £210 last Christmas.

Lisa: Not that much actually. I prefer to get lots of clothes than blow it all on one big thing.

What fashion _faux pas_ have you made?

Faye: My outfit for "5, 6, 7, 8"!

Claire: My stripy catsuit was one of them, and the bikini top in "Last Thing On My Mind" because it was too small! I go for safe things these days so I won't get caught out by old photos in the future.

Lisa: I hated my red lycra dress in "5, 6, 7, 8." One night me and Claire went out and we lost it. We didn't mean to but I felt so relieved!

H: My Flintstones jeans when I was younger were my biggest mistake.

Lee: I'm sure I've made loads. I'm not totally keyed up when it comes to fashion.

WHAT WAS YOUR FAVOURITE OUTFIT WHEN YOU WERE A KID?

Claire: I had a grey skirt and matching sweat-top with "Fame" embroidered on it. They were the best thing ever and I lived in them!

H: Some jeans with big turn-ups and a polo-neck sweater, I loved the '80s look!

Lisa: I had some jeans that I cut to just above the knee and I put a patch of material on them. I loved them because I'd made them.

Lee: Probably a football top knowing me!

Faye: I had a ra-ra dress! It was plain blue with a scooped neck and about six frills.

What's been your dodgiest hair-do?

Claire: When I had purple hair I thought it was horrible, but now when I see pictures I quite like it.

Lisa: My perm! When I was growing up it was good because I was a beauty queen and my mum used to style it for me. But I had one done last year and I hated it.

H: I had it really spiky once, and I also had the back permed. It looked so bad that I had it cut out straight away!

Faye: I've got naturally curly hair and when I was younger my mum used to brush it and I'd have the biggest hair ever! I'll sue anyone who gives a picture to the press!

Lee: When I was younger I grew my hair at the back, and I've got the fuzziest, curliest hair imaginable so it didn't grow long – it grew out!

How do you keep fit?

Lisa: I like to go dancing and swimming a lot, and I'll do sit-ups.

Faye: I'm exactly the same as Lisa.

Lee: I like to go to the gym as everybody knows, so if I've got any time I'll be in there.

H: I'm not as fit as Lee, but I try to go jogging every morning and do my sit-ups. It doesn't seem to make much difference, though!

Claire: I don't, really. I'm too lazy and I get bored if I go to the gym. I just hope that the dancing will keep me fit!

Claire: Either Jean Paul Gaultier, Gucci Envy or Issey Miyake.

Faye: I wear Envy by Gucci because it's very ladylike. But my everyday one is Aqua DiGio for men because it's fresh and lemony.

Lee: I've got loads, from Cool Water to Hugo Boss to Safari.

Lisa: I wear Hugo Boss Women because my brothers bought it for me for Christmas.

H: Jean Paul Gaultier and Hugo Boss.

THE GIRLIE STUFF!

Girls, where do you buy your make-up?

Faye: We get lots of things from MAC, and I do like Clinique, but I'm happy enough to go to Boots!

Lisa: I wear Bourgeois, MAC and Clinique – I like nice stuff!

Claire: Screenface, MAC or Boots. My stuff's either really cheap or really expensive.

What make-up item can't you live without?

Faye: Mascara, definitely.

Claire: My Touché Éclat for under my eyes, my mascara and my tweezers.

Lisa: Eyeliner and mascara.

Have you got any top make-up tips?

Faye: Always moisturise before you apply make-up.

Claire: Always put lip balm on your lips before you apply lip liner. And always have cotton buds in your make-up bag as well.

Lisa: I think eyelash curlers are brilliant because they really open your eyes.

What are your beauty secrets?

Faye: I swear by Oil of Ulay for the face, and a product called Biotherm for the body. It's amazing.

Lisa: I always cleanse and moisturise and generally take care of my skin. I think it's really important, especially as we have to wear a lot of heavy make-up.

Claire: You should drink lots of water and get lots of sleep, but I don't! But I do have a beauty routine where I cleanse and moisturise.

Lisa

When were you born?

November 5th 1975

Where were you born?

In the smallest city in the UK, St. Asaph in Wales.

What time?

8.20am

What's the naughtiest thing you did at school?

When I was about nine in junior school the headmaster sent this note to summon this boy Barry to his office. When the teacher left the classroom I got the note out of the bin and read it out to the class, and the headmaster caught me. He shouted at me so much I nearly cried!

What was the first item of clothing you bought?

Some jeans.

What was your favourite/least favourite subject at school?

My favourite was performing arts, and my least favourite was history because it was boring.

Who was your best friend?

A girl called Louise Jones who came to the Steps auditions with me.

Where did you used to hang out with your mates?

Rhuddlan Castle in Wales. We used to go exploring in the dungeons and up the old staircases and everything. It was amazing.

What was your first taste of showbiz?

I used to do lots of dancing competitions, I started when I was about seven. I loved it because I was so competitive.

Who was the first celebrity you met?

The boxer Barry McGuigan when I was 16. I told him I was going to be famous!

When did you get your ears pierced?

When I was seven. My dad said I was too young, but my mum took me anyway. Luckily my dad didn't notice for a week!

What was the first record you bought?

"Uptown Girl" by Billy Joel.

Who was your first celebrity crush on?

Michael Hutchence from INXS. I was so upset when he died.

What did you want to be when you were young?

Famous!

What colour's your bath towel at home?

Bright yellow. It's all big and fluffy and lovely.

What's your duvet like?

It's bright yellow and orange.

What's your favourite TV programme?

Eastenders.

What's your favourite kind of fish?

Prawns, and I like fish fingers!

What's your favourite flower?

Yellow tulips.

What's the most expensive thing you've ever bought?

My car. It's a Suzuki jeep that I bought off my brother.

What's your biggest regret?

I've only got one, and that's giving up playing the piano. But I'm putting that right and I'm having lessons again.

What's your biggest triumph?

Achieving my ambitions.

What makes you laugh until you cry?

H. We've been in stitches. I've laughed so much that my stomach's ached and my cheeks hurt!

Who was the last person you fancied?

Robbie Williams, although I've gone off him a bit…

What's the weirdest rumour you've heard about yourself?

There was one that me and H were an item!

How long do you take to get ready?

I can get ready in ten minutes if I want to, but it takes me ages to decide what to wear. But if I'm going somewhere special I like to take about an hour or so.

Who's your favourite Disney character?

Princess Jasmine.

What do you always carry around in your bag?

My phone and some hairspray.

How do you have your tea?

Strong and white with no sugar.

How much sleep do you need?

My average is about six hours. I like to have ten, but we never get the chance. I love sleep!

What can't you live without?

My family. They made me what I am and without them I'd be nothing.

Have you got a special teddy?

Yes, but I only started having them about a year ago. I've got loads now, and my favourite are my Rugrats because I love them.

What do you hope no-one ever finds out?

That I was a hippy in school and I went through a goth phase. I had black nails and lipstick because I wanted to look like Star out of *The Lost Boys*. My brothers disowned me!

Tell us a secret!

I've always wanted to be Baby in *Dirty Dancing*, and if they ever did a remake I would seriously go up for the part.

IT'S NOT JUST YOU LOT WHO LOVE STEPS, THE STARS CAN'T GET ENOUGH EITHER!

We Could Never Love Them More

H and Claire with B∗Witched at the Brit Awards 1999.

"I think they've got a brilliant energy and the girls' faces show great character. They look like they're kind!"
Geri Halliwell

H and Bjorn from Abba.

"I love Steps, I think they should win loads of awards because they're fantastic!"
Cerys – Catatonia

H with Zoe Ball.

"They seem really fun and you can't not dance to their music!"
Shania Twain

"They're great and I like doing all their dance routines!"
Rich – Five

"They're a really good bunch and we've had some real laughs with them, especially on the Smash Hits roadshow last year. We wish them all the best for the future!"
Bryan – Westlife

H and Lee with Steve Gately from Boyzone.

"We'd heard a lot about them back in America, then when we came to England we heard a couple of songs and they were real fun!"
AJ – Backstreet Boys

"When we performed the Abba Medley together at the Brits it was a proud moment being on stage with them. They're a lovely bunch of people and I love all their records – I sing and dance along at home before I go out!"
Tina Cousins

"They're such a fun band and they're brilliant because they don't take themselves too seriously. They just get on with it and have a laugh."
Adam Rickitt

H and Kylie.

"They're very nice people and they're so down to earth. Fame hasn't gone to their heads at all, they're just so friendly to everyone they meet. Anyone at all."
Christian – A1

"I love the energy of the group, they're just a phenomenon aren't they?"
Lee – 911

"They're such a fun group, I loved touring with them. They certainly know how to live it up!"
Lolly

"A year ago I was doing a performance in Singapore just after I finished recording… *Baby One More Time*, and I saw them and they were incredible! I'm hoping that they're going to be opening for me on my tour in America.
That would be fantastic."
Britney Spears

The guys with Boy George.

"I like Faye a lot, and I wish she was into R&B 'cos then I'd really fancy her!"
Bobak – Another Level

Robbie Williams, H and Keith Duffy from Boyzone.

117

You've got the album, you love the single, now dance along with our Step by Step guide to...

Love's Got A Hold On My Heart

1

Point both arms out in front of you.

2

With your fingers, point out, point in four times (as if saying "no")

3

4

Stick both arms out at waist level, stopping them at your sides.

Point your right hand up (with your elbow bent) and circle your hand inwards four times (still pointing).

5

Hold your right wrist with your left hand.

6

Keeping hold of your wrist, circle both arms over to the right.

7

Bring both hands back to your left side, over your heart. Brilliant! Now you've really got a hold on these moves!

8

WE TAKE A LOOK INTO THE STEPS CRYSTAL BALL

TO SEE WHAT THE FUTURE HOLDS

FOR THE FANTASTIC FIVESOME!

The Next Step... And Beyond!

The Steps story has been like a dream come true for the hardworking popsters. But what of the future? Well, for a start they're embarking on the biggest pop arena tour ever undertaken in Britain. And as anyone who saw their theatre tour will know, it's going to be brilliant. And Steps themselves can't wait.

"I think it's incredible and I'm so flattered that all those people want to come and see us." Lisa beams, "Not everybody understands what Steps is about, but if they come along they'll see that we're five young people having the time of our lives. And if people want to be a part of it, then that's great!"

Faye is just as enthusiastic. "We're extremely excited, I really can't wait. It's going to be gobsmacking. We're going to change from what we did on the theatre tour. We're going to revamp everything and make it bigger, better and more sparkly!"

And there are bound to be a few surprises in there as well. But sadly Lee's not revealing any of them! "There's going to be more of what we did on the theatre tour, and an even bigger, brighter, more fun show."

"Of course they'll be surprises, but I can't reveal what they are because otherwise they won't be surprises any more!" he says teasingly.

H IS WILLING TO GIVE A LITTLE MORE AWAY.

"WE'LL STILL BE PERFORMING ALL THE

STEPS CLASSICS, BUT MUCH MORE

BESIDES.
We'll be doing new songs off the album, we're going to have some brilliant dancers, some fantastic sets, and loads more audience participation."

We'd better start perfecting the dances routines, then!

And then there's the second album, which promises to be a huge chunk of pop genius. They've already sold a whopping 3.5 million copies of *Step One* around the world and they're still flying off the shelves! Including the singles they've sold over six million CDs in the UK alone, while "Tragedy" stayed in the charts for over six months. So do they feel a lot of pressure where the second album is concerned?

"A little bit," admits Claire, "but it's going to be even better than *Step One.* There's going to be more live sound on it, and there's even a string section in parts – I'm very excited!"

"It's going to be 100% better and even more poptastic than the first one!" Faye continues, "We can't wait to unleash it on the world!"

"It's still going to be classic Steps," H assures us, "But we're going to have lots and lots more variety on it and me and Lee are having a shot at a couple of singles as well!"

And what are the band's other hopes for the future?

"Everything!" laughs Lee.

The guys with Prince Charles at Party In The Park 1999.

"The future is exciting but quite scary because you never know what's round the corner. But we're going to keep working hard and striving. There's still so much left for us to achieve."

"WE NEVER DREAMED OR BELIEVED WE WOULD HAVE ACHIEVED ALL THIS."

Claire feels the same. "Just seeing where we can go with Steps is so important to us. But then I look at other bands out there like Boyzone and Backstreet Boys and I see how they've lasted and I hope we can do the same. And prove even more people wrong!"

They've proved wrong the millions of people who wrote them off as a one hit wonder. And as they prepare to take on new countries, they're even more determined for world domination.

As Faye says, "We're really, really looking forward to going to new countries, because every time we do it's like starting again. But we've got so much more knowledge than we had when we started out, and we know how to handle everything. We're prepared!"

Claire can't wait. "We're a little bit nervous about America because it's such a massive market and we're not your average band. But it'll be brilliant fun promo-ing there because it's larger than life." And of course, they'll be plenty of shopping opportunities. "Oh yes, I can't wait for that!" laughs Claire.

H can't get over what an amazing time they've had since they started out, and simply hopes that the success continues. "So much has happened in the last two years and it's mindblowing. As long as the next two years are as good as the last two years I'll be a very happy man."

But the final word has to go to Lisa. "We love being in Steps. Being with each other, seeing the world.

"We love having fun, so I like to think that the future is bright and positive, and we'll get bigger and better!"

Watch out the world!

THINK YOU KNOW EVERYTHING THERE IS

TO KNOW ABOUT THE SHINIEST BAND ON

PLANET POP?

Are You A Steps Superfan?

Quiz

Try our top quiz to see if you're a superfan or a superflop! Simply answer all the questions below, then add up all those you got right. You can find all the answers at the bottom of page 127. (But no cheating, now!)

1) What did Steps do to A1 on the last night of their theatre tour?

2) What's the name of the band Lisa was singing with before Steps?

3) What number did "Better Best Forgotten" get to in the charts?

4) What colour jeans did Lee wear to the Steps auditions?

5) Where was Faye born?

6) What does H dislike about Christmas?

7) What was the first record Claire bought?

8) Where did poor Lisa get stung when filming the "One For Sorrow" video?

9) Who would Lee most like to have lunch with?

10) Which famous hotel did Faye used to sing at?

11) H admits to having a really dodgy pair of jeans when he was a kid, but which cartoon characters were on the legs?

12) What did Lee want to be when he was younger?

13) What did Faye's mum used to dress her in for the beach?

14) What kind of car does Lisa own?

15) What did Claire used to spread on her toast?

16) Who's Faye's favourite Disney character?

17) What's Lee's favourite food?

18) What kind of pet does H want?

19) Which entertainment show did Claire once audition for?

20) Where did Steps film the video for "One For Sorrow"?

21) What did H sing at the Steps auditions?

22) What's Faye's favourite purchase from abroad?

23) What's Lisa's favourite Christmas present she's been given?

24) In which video does Claire wear a stripy blue catsuit?

25) What does Lee like to eat before he goes to bed?

26) What's Lisa's favourite TV programme?

27) How old was Faye when she got her ears pierced?

28) In which country did Steps have 60 bodyguards?

29) What fell on Faye during the filming of the "Better Best Forgotten" video?

30) What was Claire doing before she joined Steps?

31) What's Lee's favourite flower?

32) Where would H most love to film a video?

Seven-year-old Victoria Karageorgis is definitely a superfan! She won a competition in *The Sun* to appear in this book. Here she is with the Stepsters, along with *The Sun*'s Dominic Mohan.

33) What's the most expensive thing Faye's ever bought?

34) On which birthday did Lisa find out she'd got into Steps?

35) What was the name of Claire's former band?

36) What bizarre present did some fans once give H for Christmas?

37) What item of clothing did Claire and Lisa accidentally lose on a night out?

38) What item of make-up can't Faye live without?

39) What kind of eggs did Lee eat in Hong Kong?

40) What's the most adventurous thing H can cook?

Over 30 – Steps Superfan!

Wow! Impressive stuff! There's little you don't know about the sparkly popsters. In fact, you're 5, 6, 7, Great!

15-30 – Steps Star!

You've done your research well and you certainly know your Steps facts, but there's still room for improvement. Keep striving to be better than the best!

Under 15 – Steps Superflop!

Doh! You haven't been concentrating, now, have you? Re-read this book a million times until you've memorised every last exclamation mark and full stop!

Answers

1) Covered them in make-up and pushed them back on stage! 2) Two 3) The Lesley Curtis Affair 4) White 5) Northampton 6) His mum's gravy! 7) "Into The Groove" by Madonna 8) On the armpit 9) George Michael 10) The Hilton in London 11) Fred Flintstone and Barney Rubble 12) A footballer 13) Towelling shorts! 14) A Suzuki jeep 15) Branston pickle! 16) Tazmanian Devil 17) Spaghetti bolognese18) A puppy 19) The Barrymore Show 20) Italy 21) "Things Can Only Get Better" by D:Ream and the theme from Starlight Express 22) A miniature leather camel 23) A doll's house 24) "Last Thing On My Mind" 25) Cereal 26) Eastenders 27) 16 28) Taiwan 29) A glass wall 30) Temping as a secretary 31) Rose 32) Disney World 33) A pair of mules 34) Her 21st 35) T.S.D. 36) Some plastic cockroaches 37) Lisa's dress from the "5, 6, 7, 8" video 38) Mascara 39) Octopus! 40) Potatoes

Picture Credits